Reveal

2

HEAL

WORKING FROM THE INSIDE OUT

Reveal

2

HEAL

WORKING FROM THE INSIDE OUT

OCTAVIA BRADLEY

Get
WR TE
PUBLISHING

Reveal 2 Heal: Working from the Inside Out

Copyright © 2019 by Octavia Bradley

ISBN: 978-1-7327755-9-6

Editor: Rekesha Pittman

Cover Design: Alex Cotton, Ginisis Media

Printed in the United States of America.

Get Write Publishing
2770 Main Street – Suite 147
Frisco, TX 75033

TABLE OF CONTENTS

DEDICATION

I dedicate this book to those who are suffering in silence. It's time to break every curse that has been spoken over your life. Death can no longer grab you by the hand. Leak your secrets of trauma. You are no longer trapped by the strongholds of your past. You are not alone, God is with you and I am here for you.

Remember that God loves you. I love you. Now it's time for **you** to love you.

"Commit your works to the Lord and your thoughts will be established."

- Proverbs 16:3 (NKJV)

FOREWORD

I love the 8th verse of Psalm 4: *"In peace I will both lie down and sleep, for you alone, oh Lord, will keep me safe."* Today, I can claim that verse to be my personal experience, that is, when at the end of the day, I lay my head on the pillow, I go to sleep in peace. However, there was a time in my life when that wasn't the case. It was a time of holding on to the pain of my past. Pain that influenced my poor choices during the day and the pain that robbed me of sleep at night. There was nowhere to hide from the pain in my life and worst of all, there was no peace.

God has used my lifelong craft of carpentry to illustrate similarities in the process of rebuilding a home to the process of healing from the pain of your past. For example, during a typical renovation, the first thing you are required to do is demolition. You must get rid of any and all rot and decay before you can begin installing anything new. It just wouldn't make sense to install new product on top of what had been rotting and decaying for years, would it? It would simply be a matter of time before the new product would become contaminated by the rot and decay left in place beneath the new installations. It's no different as you try to get past the pain of your past.

People want to rebuild their shattered lives without doing the demolition work crucial to removing the rot and decay of the past, and when they do, everything new they try to build is destroyed by the underlying, unaddressed trauma (rot) and pain (decay) of the past.

Octavia Bradley's inspiration for R.E.V.E.A.L. 2 H.E.A.L. was birthed from a place of personal pain. For that reason, she can speak and teach on this topic in ways that others cannot. I consider R.E.V.E.A.L. 2 H.E.A.L. to be the 21st Century "How-To" blueprint for both addressing the pain of your past and experiencing victory over it Octavia's authentic transparency and courage to R.E.V.E.A.L. (demolition) real-life trauma will without question empower others to H.E.A.L. from personal trauma in ways they could have never imagined. You simply cannot do what this book says to do and not experience transformation!

"…but be transformed by the renewal of your mind…"
- Romans 12:2

-Mike Palombi

ACKNOWLEDGEMENTS

I am thankful for the tears, pain and laughter I endured through the journey I traveled.

I thank God for writing my book of life, allowing me to be a victim and creating me to be a warrior for His people.

I thank my husband for considering me to be worth fighting for.

I am thankful to my children for teaching me patience, kindness, and love.

I also want to thank my supporters and mentors who not only stuck by my side but who have helped me grow through this process of healing.

Finally, I thank YOU for journeying beyond your past and embracing your future.

PREFACE

Reveal 2 Heal developed from my very personal experiences with abuse, abandonment, drugs, sex, faith, healing, obedience, and love. I held on to the statement, "What happens in this house stays in this house" every day of my life.

I was broken by those I loved daily. I no longer knew who I was or who I was to become. I just had passion in my heart to serve God's people by working with families who had been through similar or worse experiences.

It wasn't until I felt the love of a man who thought I was worth fighting for that I decided to fight for myself. I decided to Recognize and Release Each Vicious Episode Attacking Life 2 Help Every Aspiration Live. This process has tested, lifted, stretched, and embraced me, allowing me to understand and accept that I can do all things through Christ who strengthens me.

INTRODUCTION

Having held on to secrets for so long, I am a voice you want to hear and read about. In my auto-biography *Leaked: Spilling Secrets of Trauma*, I took the statement, "What happens in this house stays in this house," and released the most painful and traumatic secrets about my family and myself. I could no longer be bound to the strongholds of my past because they were constantly getting in the way of my future. I have given everyone else power and authority over my life for the past 30 years.

Can you imagine how that may feel? Every day of my life I struggled with fear, poor self-esteem, depression, suicidal thoughts, hopelessness, in-security, worthlessness, anxiety, post-traumatic stress and pain—both mentally and emotionally.

I did not want to be a parent. I often showed two faces—a smile that gave other people life, happiness and hope, and a frown that emanated from the inside of me and surfaced as a monster behind closed doors. I gave those closest to me sadness and despair. I was so busy being fake and gave all the love I had within to others. I couldn't see that I needed love myself.

Loving yourself is crucial to living life because it can destroy or revive anyone, including you.

Love is an emotion that can play tricks on your mind, body and soul.

At times, we live each day according to our feelings. If we don't live according to our feelings, we live in the shadow of our past experiences of hurt, abuse and pain. On this journey, I will share the road I decided to take to get my life back in order and become who I was created to be and to do what I was put on earth to do—R.E.V.E.A.L. 2 H.E.A.L.! Recognize and Release Every Vicious Episode Attacking Life 2 Help Every Aspiration Live! I call these powerful words the laws of self, working from the inside out.

Though my life story is mine, I am sure there is a piece of you hidden in the episodes of your past that can relate to my journey. I just pray that my story will help you find the strength to be honest with yourself and reveal the secrets of your past that are stopping you from becoming the *real* you.

PART ONE

PART
ONE

Chapter 1

UNDERSTANDING LAWS: WHY DO WE NEED THEM?

Laws were made to keep order amongst people to show uniformity and provide guidelines that everyone could live by, with a promise of repercussions if a law was broken. Ironic as it may seem, laws were made to be broken because of the sinful nature of humans. Though God knew we were sinful beings, that didn't stop God from choosing us. God created commandments for us to follow and gave His only begotten Son to die for our sins.

The Ten Commandments:

1. You shall have no other Gods but me.
2. You shall not make for yourself any idol, nor bow down to it or worship it.
3. You shall not misuse the name of the Lord your God.
4. You shall remember and keep the Sabbath day holy.
5. Respect your father and mother.
6. You must not commit murder.
7. You must not commit adultery.
8. You must not steal.

9. You must not give false evidence against your neighbor.

10. You must not be envious of your neighbor's goods. You shall not be envious of his house nor his wife, nor anything that belongs to your neighbor.

I know what you may be thinking… *why was the law created if people were going to break them anyway?* Or why did God give His only Son, knowing the nature of His people? I will answer your second question first. God loved us as stated in John 3:16; "For God so loved the world, that He gave His only begotten Son, that whosoever believeth in him should not perish, but have everlasting life." In response to the first question, the commandments were established for the people and their personal well-being.

This does not mean that we are saved by these commandments, it means that we can live life more abundantly with integrity and honor. If God provided us with laws to live a better life, why can't we govern ourselves accordingly? It is time to R.E.V.E.A.L. what is preventing us from H.E.A.L.ing and become what God created us to be.

Since people need something or someone to follow, why not set laws for yourself and live by **your** promise to create a new you each day of your life? If you are ready to R.EV.E.A.L. 2

H.E.A.L., turn to the next page. If not, please close this book until you become ready. It's time to let go now!

Psalm 40:8

**I delight to do Your will, O my God,
And Your Law is within my heart.**

Chapter 2

R-RECOGNIZE AND RELEASE

Did you ever find yourself in a position where you had to make all of the decisions, but you were not old enough to make them? Were you ever abused physically, mentally, verbally, or emotionally by a loved one or someone you trusted? Were you ever sexually abused, sexually assaulted, or molested? Were you ever told to be quiet about what went on in your house or told not to tell because no one would believe you? Have your ever thought about harming yourself or others because you could no longer bear the pain? Were you bullied, humiliated, tortured, or forced to do things against your will to show how much you loved someone? Have you lashed out at a loved one because you were unable to control how you felt? Are you impulsive? Have you ever been abandon-ed? Are you wearing a mask? Do you know what it feels like to love yourself?

If you said yes to any of these questions you have taken the first step in recognizing the pain that is buried within. To be able to **recognize** means you are identifying and acknowledging your truth.

When I first started writing my autobiography, I could not believe I was writing down the secrets

I was warned to never tell. I started writing about the molestation that began at the age of 5, to the abuse I endured for 10 years at the hands of my ex-husband. I had to realize that I was not put on this earth to remain trapped, I was placed here to be free. Through my writing I let go of my vulnerability, embarrassment, pride, and the humiliation I carried. I **released**, which means to set free or escape from confinement. In my case, I was confined in my mind, body and emotions.

I gave people who hurt me, harmed me, abused me, humiliated me, belittled me, damaged me, and broke me power over my life. People controlled my emotions, my thoughts, the way I perceived things, and the way I lived.

I would repeat cycles of abuse by doing a majority of these things to others that were done to me. I would yell and curse at my children and beat my children when they did something wrong. It wasn't an ordinary beating, it was corporal punishment with belts, hangers, or shoes. I would embarrass my so-called friends and make them feel stupid or inferior. I would treat people unfairly and talk about people behind their backs. I even would hit my partner, thinking that would get him to listen to me and love me. This is not how you should live. The people around you should not accept abusive behavior and you should not accept mistreatment from anyone.

In drug recovery programs, counselors would say, "People, places and things can bring you down." You must learn to recognize the people, places, and things that stir up negative feelings that cause you to react in an unhealthy way. Release everything that stops you from being free.

In order to release something, there is a choice that must be made. You have already made a choice by reading this book. The pain that you feel remains because you are allowing yourself to hold on. You must now allow yourself to let go. Make the choice to love yourself more, regardless of what you have been exposed to in the past.

When I wrote *Leaked: Spilling Secrets of Trauma*, I had to make a choice to be free. Everyone has a story to tell and the only people that heal from their stories are the ones who reveal them. Your past does not define you, so get out of your own way. Create an atmosphere of true love for yourself and for those around you. You can do this! Continue to recognize and release, knowing that you are not alone.

Remember, you can do all things do Christ who strengthens you. (Philippians 4:13). Here are some steps to get you through your first law of working from the inside out.

RECOGNIZE & RELEASE PRAYER

Father God, in the name of Jesus, I come thanking You for the life I have journeyed thus far. I thank You for all You have done for me and all You are doing for me.

Lord God, I ask for You to help me recognize each painful experience that has hindered me from being the person You have called me to be. I ask that You help me face the barriers of my past and forgive those who have caused me harm.

Lord, I am unable to complete this process by myself. I ask that You release me from the toxicity of old wounds, memories, struggles, sadness and hurt. I ask that You show me how to release the old me and embrace the new me. Please surround me with more of You, happiness, success, love and understanding in order to do Your will. I am ready to do a great work starting with me.

In Jesus' Mighty Name, Amen.

STEPS

Here are steps to get you through your first law working from the inside out.

1. Begin your day with prayer and talk to God. Tell Him your pain, fears, and most importantly, your past. Though God knows all about it, tell Him in your words and in your voice.
2. Listen to the song "Better" by Jessica Reedy. Allow the words to sink in and stretch you. Listen to this song daily.
3. Breathe in through your nose and out through your mouth for five to ten minutes.
4. Mediate on your first scripture of strength. Philippians 4:13 (I can do all things through Christ who strengthens me) day and night for at least 21 days.
5. Write down the things you have hidden from yourself and note any past experiences that have harmed or hindered you. Record any things you didn't like or made you feel sad and unsure.
6. Congratulations, your new chapter has begun!

Dear Old Me,

People, Places Things:

I won't go back, so why are you here? What you did to me could never compare to the years that you stole. To have me unfold, truth be told, I'm the victor. You've been sold to the highest bidder who let you unleash the beast within and watched you roam the streets to seek the warrior that you thought you'd defeat.

Here I am now—the new me. I'll decree to the people, places and things I once feared, you helped make me stronger. Yeah, that's what you did. I'm saying bye to the old me, you see. If you don't get it, I have victory!

Chapter 3

E-EACH

Remembering each painful event in my life made me feel like giving up. Why did I want to recall each painful experience? I believe it was because remembering gave me back power over my life.

Holding on to each person that caused me pain left me numb in parts of my body, mind, and spirit. The word **each** refers to every person, place, or thing regarded and identified separately. Being able to compartmentalize each person, place, or thing helped me to REVEAL what I was truly going through. Making a list of each person, place, and thing has also helped me recognize and work through potential triggers that would have resurfaced in my future.

When I met my husband, he showered me with love. He showed me what it meant to really love someone and how it felt to receive love. Each man that I had come across prior to my husband gave me their own interpretation of love that I accepted because I knew nothing else.

I reached a point in my life where I needed each part of me to unite and be strong. I needed to connect with the battered, broken child hiding inside of the body of a so-called polished woman.

"Lovingkindness and truth met together;
righteousness and peace have kissed each other."
- Psalm 82:10

I reference this scripture because lovingkindness means to have tenderness and consideration and truth means to be honest with fact or reality. If I am going to let my guard down with myself, I must allow the truth to set me free. I allowed righteousness (my past experiences and pain) and peace (my thoughts to seek a new me) to kiss each other and mend a relationship that need reconciliation.

Can you name each of your painful experiences and break them down into, people, places or things? Yes, you can! Allow Psalm 85:10 to be your guide and lift each category into prayer, no matter how long it may take for you to do so.

PRAYER FOR EACH PERSON, PLACE OR THING

Father God, in the name of Jesus, I come to You thanking You for all I have been through. Lord, You are amazing and You are the Great I Am.

Lord, I humbly ask You to show me each person, place, or thing and help me to see the truth and work through my pain. Lord, I cannot do it without You. I don't want to go back to the old me.

Lord God, Your Word says "Create in me a clean heart and renew a right spirit in me" (Psalm 51:10). I am ready to accept my part and work in the glory of Your grace and mercy.

In Jesus' Name, Amen!

STEPS

Here are steps to get you through your second law working from the inside out.

1. Begin your day with prayer and talk to God. Tell Him your thoughts about this new process. Though God knows all about it, tell Him from your words and in your voice.
2. Write down each person, place, or thing that has caused you harm or made you feel unworthy.
3. Listen to the song "Flow" by Jessica Reedy. Allow the words to sink in and stretch you. Listen to this song daily.
4. Breathe in through your nose and out through your mouth for five to ten minutes.
5. Mediate on your second scripture of reconciliation - Psalm 85:10 (Lovingkindness and truth met together; righteousness and peace have kissed each other) day and night for at least 21 days. Bonus scripture: Psalm 51:10 "Create in me a clean heart, O God and renew a right spirit within me."
6. Congratulations, you made it through another phase of R.E.V.E.A.L.

Dear Emotions,

Intent:

How did I let you enslave me so quickly? Your loved turned from kindness to insults and hits. The treasure I carried, buried deep within, I could no longer show, because I sinned.

I became you, which was really your intent for me be to cruel and filled with violence. My response from the pain that cluttered my brain, the broken and the battered became a potion. I will treat everyone how you did me—I'll lie, I'll cheat and become shifty. No one seemed to love the good girl anyway. My intent was to hurt you and just walk away.

Little did I know, there was another plan in play. God's intent would not let me continue to stray. I had to repent, and walk in the straight, bounce back, and get refocused today.

I had to walk the path to the other side where my destiny awaited. The real purpose of my life could no longer be faked.

Chapter 4

V-VICIOUS

The first time I became pregnant, I had no idea. I was very naïve and was not focused on my body the way I should have been. I found out I was pregnant because of the man I was married to at that time. He looked at my naked body in the mirror and said, "You are pregnant." I looked at him with excitement in my eyes as if to say *how do you know?* He said, "Look how big your breasts are. It's a girl; you're not keeping it." I know what you are thinking, *how did he know this?* Was he right? Unfortunately, he was.

I do not know if it was a girl or not, but he forced me to get an abortion. He kicked me in the stomach and pushed me to the floor. Each time I became pregnant, the same thing happened until 2002 when he sensed I was having a boy and allowed me to keep it.

Being cruel or violent is the definition of **vicious**. Remembering each person, place, or thing has allowed me to focus on the nature of people including myself. I too, at some points in my life became just as cruel and violent as the people I remember.

There is a vicious cycle of fear and immobility that develops within people who have suffered from traumatic experiences. Fear is what keep us immobile and traps us mentally and emotionally in a dark hole of trauma.

Think about what you go through when you feel like there is no way out. Think about how your body reacts. You go through the arousal state, which allows your body to sense the danger you are in, known as your fight or flight response. Those feelings and/or thoughts become trapped. Then, you meet the unsuccessful escape phase, which allows your body to tattoo the reasons behind those feelings in your body's nervous system.

You arrive at the next phase of helplessness because of the fear you experienced. This causes you to settle for what has been done and not acknowledge it. Instead, you bury it within, leaving yourself open for the final phase of immobility.

Immobility is a response that is difficult to stop because of the powerful emotional energy of fear and dread that hold the nervous system captive. This vicious cycle of fear prevents you from responding in a healthy and positive way. This leads to post-traumatic stress disorder or similar consequences.

Ask yourself, what vicious cycles of fear have you inflicted on others? Be honest, it's only you and God. Remember, He knows all but still wants you to come to Him. God will forgive you, but the truth of the matter is, you must forgive yourself. The Bible says, "Hatred stirs up strife, but love covers all offenses" (Proverbs 10:12). If you are dwelling on your pain and the things or people who caused it, you are going to be filled with hatred.

Hatred will manifest itself in every part of your body and cause you to become bitter from the inside out. It will become a mask of pain, anger, sorrow, frustration, bitterness, deceit and rage. You will not let that happen. You will work from within.

Recognize and Release Each Vicious Episode Attacking Life! Demonstrate the love you have inside. Do not allow anger, hatred and past experiences to resurface and control how you move and think. Instead, allow love to flood your heart with forgiveness, joy, laughter and peace. This does not mean that you will forget the pain, it means when the pain tries to resurface and control you, the love you have trained your body to give will block those receptors from entertaining the pain.

PRAYER

Father God in the name of Jesus, I come before You to give You thanks. Thank You for allowing me to see another day. Thank You for my family and those You have placed in my life.

Father God, I thank You for allowing me to recognize the vicious cycles that I have repeated knowingly and unknowingly. Lord, I ask for Your continued guidance. I ask that You deliver me from every cruel thought, feeling or action within. Lord God, I ask that You hold me accountable for my actions and allow me to repent at the moment of sin. Lord, I ask that You teach me and help me to love unconditionally, starting with myself. God, I adhere to Your Word, because You are awesome, You are magnificent, You are the great I AM, You are Marvelous, You are my God.

In Jesus name,
Amen.

STEPS

1. Begin your day with prayer and talk to God. Tell Him your thoughts about removing the old you and wanting to be made over. Though God knows all about it, tell Him from your words and in your voice.
2. Write down how you believe you have hurt people, focusing on the reasons you hurt them. If you can, seek forgiveness from them directly.
3. Listen to the song "My Hands Are Lifted Up/Make Me Over" by Brianna Babineaux. Allow the words to sink in and stretch you. Allow the song to minister to you. Receive it and listen to this song daily.
4. Breathe in through your nose and out through your mouth for 10 to 15 minutes.
5. Mediate on your third scripture of love with self. Proverbs 85:10 "Hatred stirs up strife, but love covers all offenses" day and night for at least 21 days.

Congratulations, you made it through a phase of surrender!

For the Abuser:

Torture

I am tortured because I am helpless. I am still because I am shocked. I am quiet because you told me not to tell and I am fearful because I dwell.

In the moments I am still, only to have thoughts to kill. Not you, ironically, just the caged bird inside of me. You took away the innocence I had, with a touch, a rape, a smile or a dial.

Don't you feel bad? How many victims have you made sad? Today is the day I will expose, not you, but the feelings of death in my episode.

Chapter 5

E-EPISODE

The cuts I administered to myself felt good. I felt free of any pain I felt prior to me cutting myself. Taking a whole bottle of pills made me sleep and dream about stillness. The alcohol I drank every day made me forget the reason why I started drinking in the first place. Drinking brought me to life. I was a different person and everyone loved me as an alcoholic, or so I thought.

I no longer wanted to live. I was throwing my life away all because I was trapped by experiences filled with pain. My body couldn't tell the difference and kept accepting the pain because I never told a soul about my episodes. **Episode** is the infinite period in which someone is affected by a specified illness. In my case, depression was my illness.

Yes, I suffered from depression. There are many episodes in my life that I can share with you, but the one that impacted who I was and who I was to become happened under the episodes of depression. Unbeknownst to me, I suffered from depression at an early age. It started from being molested. My body held on to the emotions of a 5-year-old who couldn't understand why love (my so-called family) hurt me. Those emotions appeared again and again, each time more terrifying than the last.

I am a victim of any type of abuse you can imagine, caused by the people I loved and trusted, including myself. Out of every person I can blame, I must take responsibility for my reactions. I did not have faith in God to love myself; instead, I tried to kill myself. He created me for a purpose. How do I know this? I am still here after all I have been through and it is not by chance. What God has in store for you can't be undone.

Don't allow your depressive state to sabotage your life. Continue the journey to R.E.V.E.A.L. your pain. The episodes of your life are segments of stories that have affected you both good and bad; however, we tend to hold on to the bad rather than holding on to the good.

Episodes can show themselves at the most crucial times in our lives and leave us paralyzed. It is up to us to choose what happens next. Allow your memory to unfold. Face the pain from the inside out. You can do it because you were created with strength.

Remember, the Bible has 66 episodes (books), each with different stories to tell. Once your story is told, it's up to you to move forward in forgiveness or remain in bitterness. Psalm 139:29-24 says "Search me, O God, and know my heart; Try me, and know my anxieties; And see if *there is any* wicked way in me and lead me in the way of everlasting." What episode are you willing to share to be led in the way of healing?

PRAYER

Father God, in the name of Jesus, I come before You to give You thanks. Father, I need You more now than ever before. I have remembered the episodes of my life that have affected me the most and I need Your guidance. I need Your love and arms to hold me when I am weak.

Lord, Your Word says that You will never leave me nor forsake me. I trust You, Lord. Father God, I know I am in a place of pain, yearning to have it lifted. I ask You right now in the name of Jesus, to remove each bitter feeling I have. I ask You to remove any thoughts that are not of You. I ask that You convict my heart and remove each foul word from my vocabulary. Father God, I thank You for allowing me to come face-to-face with the episodes of my past, both buried and alive.

Lord God, I ask for Your continued guidance. I ask that You free me from every cruel thought, feeling or act within. Lord, I ask that You hold me accountable for my actions and allow me to repent at the moment of sin. Lord, please help me to love unconditionally, starting with myself. Lord God, I adhere to Your Word, because You are awesome, You are magnificent, You are the Great I AM, You are Marvelous, You are my God.

In Jesus name,
Amen.

STEPS

1. Begin your day with prayer and talk to God. Tell Him your thoughts about removing the old you and wanting to be made over. Though God knows all about it, tell him from your words and in your voice.
2. Write down the hidden episodes of your heart.
3. Listen to the song "Praying" by Kesha. Allow the words to sink in and stretch you wide. Allow the song to minister to you. Receive it and listen to this song daily.
4. Breathe in through your nose and out through your mouth for 10 to 15 minutes.
5. Mediate on your fourth scripture to help you acknowledge the episodes of pain and guidance into salvation. Psalm 139:23-24 says "Search me, O God, and know my heart; Try me, and know my anxieties; And see if *there is any* wicked way in me and lead me in the way of everlasting love with self."

Read Psalm 139

O LORD, You have examined my heart and know everything about me. You know when I sit down or stand up. You know my thoughts even when I'm far away. You see me when I travel and when I rest at home. You know everything I do. You know what I am going to say even before I say it, LORD. You go before me and follow me. You place Your hand of blessing on my head. Such knowledge is too wonderful for me, too great for me to understand! I can never escape from Your Spirit! I can never get away from Your presence! If I go up to heaven, You are there; if I go down to the grave, You are there. If I ride the wings of the morning, if I dwell by the farthest oceans, even there Your hand will guide me, and Your strength will support me. I could ask the darkness to hide me and the light around me to become night—but even in darkness I cannot hide from You. To You the night shines as bright as day. Darkness and light are the same to You. You made all the delicate, inner parts of my body and knit me together in my mother's womb. Thank You for making me so wonderfully complex! Your workmanship is marvelous—how well I know it. You watched me as I was being formed in utter seclusion, as I was woven together in the dark of the womb. You saw me before I was born. Every day of my life was recorded in Your book. Every moment was laid out before a single day had passed. How precious are Your thoughts about me, O God. They cannot be numbered! I can't even count them; they outnumber the grains of sand! And when I wake up, You are still with me! O God, if only You would destroy the wicked! Get out of my life, you murderers! They blaspheme You; Your enemies misuse Your name. O LORD, shouldn't I hate those who hate You? Shouldn't I despise those who oppose You? Yes, I hate them with total hatred, for Your enemies are my enemies. Search me, O God, and know my heart; test me and know my anxious thoughts. Point out anything in me that offends You and lead me along the path of everlasting life.

Congratulations, you made it through a phase of memory!

Dear Enemy,

Sickness:

I am weak, my head is bursting with pain. It started in my eyes. Am I really insane? Now it's my neck, it feels hot, then cold. Nevermind… the pain just moved to my bones. Oh, no! This is it. I'm having sharp pains like fangs in my neck.

Oh yes, I'm insane. Pains in my chest, in my legs, I am weak. I keep walking straight, but can't see beyond me.

I feel a tap on my shoulder and I jump back with fear. Then I hear someone say, "My child, you are here." I brought you through the storm because you're warring for my people. You had to live by example, so that you can be equal. People won't believe if you hadn't been victim. Now your story is theirs and you can reach them.

Put on your armor of God and stand strong, because you have been equipped all along. Tell the enemy to flee, he is not welcomed here. Now, I loose your mind from all despair. Stand strong in your faith, as the battle is won. You're here in victory, standing in the Sun.

Chapter 6

A-ATTACKING

Heart palpitations came and went each day and I never understood why. As a young girl, I always complained that this or that was bothering me internally. I would get headaches and was told that I needed glasses—not by an optician, but my foster parent. Funny how she never took me to get what she said I needed.

I would get sharp stabbing pains in my chest and stomach. My exact words were, "I think I am dying." I was told to stop saying that and to go sit down or, "You are dying alright, because you're bad."

In my teenage years, I stopped complaining so much and stopped using those words. Little did I know, I was slowly dying within. I didn't know how to express myself beyond the attacks I had made on my body. I numbed myself with pain; using a razor blade, a knife, an iron, sex, drugs, alcohol, and self-doubt. I didn't love myself and I didn't know how to. I relied on the so-called love that others showed me, but after some time I realize they were attacking me. **Attack** means acting against someone or something aggressively in attempt to injure or kill. I was attacked by everyone, including me.

Years later, I learned that a lot of the ailments people have today is because of their history. No, I don't mean because it was passed down through the heredity of family genes. I mean it was passed down from the trauma a person holds onto. The trauma or pained experiences that we think we have buried or tossed aside and moved on with our lives are just our innate characteristics (fight or flight response), our defense mechanism, or our great escape.

Trauma Transference Syndrome (TTS) is real. TTS is a traumatic experience that impacts the entire person including the way you think, the way you learn, the way you remember things, the way you feel about yourself, the way you feel about other people, and the way you make sense of the world. If trauma is not processed, the powerful images, feelings, and sensations do not just go away; instead, they are deeply imprinted and stored in the body's cellular memory.

Have you heard the statement "mind over body?" It's willing the mind to do what the body does not want to. Have you heard the statement, I over E, or intelligence over emotions? It means to think with your brain and not with your feelings (your heart). These statements are true; however, if you have a life of unsettled emotions it is hard to adapt to these statements.

Unsettled emotions affect our bodies in the form of sickness, which include but are not limited to high blood pressure, gastrointestinal symptoms, chronic pain, fibromyalgia, migraines, addictions, and certain cancers. Think about your pain and sicknesses throughout the years. Why did it form? Better yet, what did it come from?

It's time to take back your life by taking control of your mind and your body. Watch what you put into your body by way of food, music, television, gossip, the environment you share, the words that you speak against yourself and others, and the things you read.

You must show your body love and affection. You must surround yourself with positivity and remember to release any person, place or thing that is not positive. Now, what does that look like? We can live life thinking we are in a positive situation because it's all we know and we consider it to be normal—like beating our children with belts and cords, slapping their faces, cursing and yelling at them, or calling them stupid and dumb. Is this normal because it happened to you, or you saw your parents or grandparents do the same thing? Why are we enslaved to pain and abuse? This is not normal.

Ask yourself, "Am I truly happy? What improvements do I need to make in my life, starting on the inside? Do I smile because I am happy and thankful? Do I trust myself, or better yet, do I *know* myself? Am I genuinely happy for others? Do I encourage others or tear them down? Am I living life on purpose or am I merely existing? I know that these are a lot of questions, but you must be honest with yourself. Level up, it's healing time.

Remember, love suffers long *and* is kind; love does not envy; love does not parade itself, is not puffed up; does not behave rudely, does not seek its own, is not provoked, thinks no evil; does not rejoice in iniquity, but rejoices in the truth; bears all things, believes all things, hopes all things, endures all things (1 Corinthians 13:4-7).

PRAYER

Father God, in the name of Jesus, I come before You to give You thanks. Father, You have shown me the way, the truth, and the light.

I declare and decree that I am not going to stop working on me from the inside out. I declare and decree that I will live on purpose. I declare and decree that I will not be stagnated by the strongholds of my past. I declare and decree that nothing shall stop me and my cup will run over. I declare and decree that I will seek You first. I declare and decree that the cycles of bondage are broken.

I am not a mistake and trials of my journey were worth my rebirth. I need You more now than ever before. I ask You right now in the name of Jesus to lift my burdens and allow me to do Your work wholeheartedly.

In Jesus' Name, Amen!

STEPS

1. Begin your day with prayer and talk to God. Tell Him your thoughts about removing the old you and wanting to be made over. Though God knows all about it, tell Him from your words and in your voice.
2. Write down the hidden episodes of your heart.
3. Listen to the song "Fill Me Up" by Tasha Cobbs. Allow the words to sink in and stretch you. Allow the song to minister to you. Receive it and listen to this song daily.
4. Breathe in through your nose and out through your mouth for 15 to 20 minutes.
5. Focus on the thoughts and feelings that have formed in your mind and heart.
6. Smile at someone you don't know today, just because! Remember, your energy is of love and excitement.
7. Mediate on your 5th scripture to help you love yourself and others with a pure heart. Love suffers long *and* is kind; love does not envy; love does not parade itself, is not puffed up; does not behave rudely, does not seek its own, is not provoked, thinks no evil; does not rejoice in iniquity, but rejoices in the truth; bears all things, believes all things, hopes all things, endures all things, (1st Corinthians 13:4-7)

Dear Death,

Sorry NOT Sorry:

You thought you had me, you tried to take me out, but He had other plans for my life, no doubt. No more sitting and waiting for you to intervene, I'm living life for me and there could be no in-between. Now, I know that you're mad. I'm sorry, NOT sorry! Here is the truth: you always sabotaged me. No matter what my intuition said, I never walked away. Truth be told, I should be dead. Living life after life, and chance after chance. My Savior died for me so I can live again.

Chapter 7

L-LIFE

Life has its ups and downs. For me, it seemed as though there were more downs than ups. Despite it all, I would not change it for the world.

This is my journey, my story, and my reward. I have become closer to God and I have faith larger than a mustard seed. Life for me did not begin when I was born on May 11th but when I began seeking God for myself and listening to His voice. I started surrounding myself with people who were about my Father's business. My conversation and my thought process transformed. I started standing on my own and acknowledged who am I according to the Word of God. I am full of life and I am truly living.

Life is defined as the existence of a human being. Existence means continued survival. When you look at your own life, you should know that you survived despite the odds that were stacked against you. Know that your battles were yours. You overcame what most people would have ended their life for. You must continue to live, but not in the same way you did merely to survive. You must not live for others. It's your time to live life for yourself! In doing so, understand that you have the victory because God gave His only begotten Son to die for you.

The only way to live your life in the path of righteous is by conforming your heart and transforming your mind according to God's will. This will help you to gain insight about your purpose. This does not mean you will be 100% perfect; however, you will strive to live each day on purpose and with perfect peace. Your journey from this point on will never be the same because you now know that the enemy's goal is to make your life hell.

Are you going to give the enemy power over your life? I didn't think so. Let's join forces and allow the healing process to begin. Remember, your mess will be your message.

PRAYER

Lord God, I come before you today, asking You for nothing but thanking You for everything. Thank You, God, for lifting me up. Thank You for saving me from myself and the hands of the enemy. Thank You for showing me that the battle is not mine it's Yours.

Thank You for trusting me to be the voice for your people. Thank You, Lord, for not letting me die physically and for reviving me with every aspect of life. Thank You, Lord, for the stories before me. Thank You for the family you have given me. Thank You for the opportunities You have set before me. Thank You for calling me. Lord, I will do Your will.

In Jesus' Name, Amen.

STEPS

1. Begin your day with prayer and talk to God. Tell Him your thoughts about how good He is in your life and how you want to do His great work in others. Yes, He knows your heart but tell Him using your voice.

2. Write down the transformation you see in yourself. Write down the transformation you see in your circle. Many times, your circle can be a reflection of you.

3. Listen to the song "Praying" by Kesha. Allow the words to sink in and stretch you. Allow the song to minister to you. Receive it and listen to this song daily.

4. Breathe in through your nose and out through your mouth for 15 to 20 minutes.

5. Focus on the thoughts and feelings that have formed in your mind and heart.

6. Smile at someone you don't know today, just because! Remember, your energy is of love and excitement.

7. Start a positive conversation with someone you don't know.

8. Reach out to someone who has caused you pain and tell them you forgive them. You can write a letter, make a call, or send a text—just make the connection.

9. Meditate on your previous scriptures daily. Allow each scripture to provide life and under-

standing, acceptance, forgiveness, and new energy.

10. Mediate on your sixth scripture to help you love yourself and others with a pure heart and to forgive and release any toxicity within (Ephesians 4:31-32). Get rid of all bitterness, rage, anger, harsh words, or slander, as well as all types of evil behavior. Be kind to one other, tenderhearted, forgiving one another, just as God through Christ has forgiven you.

PART
TWO

Chapter 8

THE UNION OF PEACE BETWEEN TO ENTITIES

You have made it through the R.E.V.E.A.L. (Recognize & Release Each Vicious Episode Attacking Life) process. What are you feeling and thinking at this point in your life?

_____

_____

_____

_____

_____

_____

_____

_____

_____

You have transitioned from secrecy and leaked your innermost thoughts and feelings that were holding you back. You have become honest with yourself and with others. You are now able to face who you were and become who you are destined to be!

In the Bible it states where two or three are gathered in my name I am there amongst them (Mathew 18:20). The number 2 is very significant in the in the Bible. It has a few meanings including *unity*, or *union*. Union as in marriage bringing two people together and uniting them as one (Genesis 2:22-25).

This is your process. You have faced your past head on and with honesty. You have unlocked and broken the strongholds of your past. You have journeyed on the road less traveled by stepping out on faith. You have married yourself and promised to love yourself unconditionally. You have united with the old you to get to the new you. Are you seeing this process? You are here on purpose living for the days to come and not for the days that were. You are free! It's time to H.E.A.L.

THE UNION OF PEACE

REFLECTIONS

_____

_____

_____

_____

_____

_____

_____

_____

_____

_____

_____

_____

REFLECTIONS

_____

_____

_____

_____

_____

_____

_____

_____

_____

_____

_____

_____

Chapter 9

H-HELP

Think positive. Whatever you put your mind to, you can do. Write the vision and make it plain. This is your time to do your very best. I love me. I forgave me. I am strong. I will surround myself with people who treat me well. I am a better person.

Helping others is the easiest task for you but helping yourself is even easier. Making it through this healing process will take some time, and you will make it.

To **help** means to improve a situation or problems. You are improving on everything in your life. You are making a change that is worth the fight.

Put on the whole armor of God, starting with prayer. Begin your day in prayer to help you to stand firm on God's Word. Have faith, leaving all matters that you face daily in His hands.

Your Helmet of Salvation will rescue you from your own mess. Understand that salvation has been given to you through Jesus Christ. Always protect what enters your mind. Surround yourself with God's Word, a positive environment, and good thoughts.

The Belt of Truth allows us to be strengthened by God's Word and helps us to stand firm and confident. The Breastplate of Righteousness is the covering of God's righteousness protecting the heart from the enemy and deception. The Gospel of Peace is worn on our feet, allowing us to be ready for each area in our lives knowing "It is freedom that Christ has set us free. Stand firm, and do not let yourselves be burdened again by a yoke of slavery" (Galatians 5:1). The Shield of Faith allows us to stand firm when we are being attacked, shielding all the blows of the enemy. "No weapon formed against you shall prosper, and every tongue which rises against you in judgment you shall condemn" (Isaiah 54:17). The Sword of the Spirit is the Word of God through which we are to live by.

PRAYER

Lord God, please allow me to continue to do a great work. I declare and decree that no weapon formed against me shall prosper. I declare and decree that I will surround myself with positivity and bind any negative spirits that try to enter my spirit.

I declare and decree that I will live my life according to Your Word. I declare and decree that I will not fall back into the old me. I declare and decree that I have the tools necessary for the new me to succeed.

I declare and decree that I will change my thinking and my attitude towards others. I declare and decree that I will seek Your face daily and listen for Your response. I declare and decree that I am worth fighting for and I am worth saving. I declare that my decrees are not just words, but faith in action. Thank You, Lord, for loving me and being God Almighty.

In Jesus' Name, Amen.

STEPS

1. Begin your day with prayer and talk to God.
2. Place positive affirmations around your house.
3. Look at yourself in the mirror and smile.
4. Write down two short-term goals you want to accomplish in the next two weeks.
5. Listen to the song "The Call" by Isabella Davis. Allow the words to sink in and stretch you. Allow the song to minister to you. Receive it and listen to this song daily.
6. Run in place for two minutes at your own speed.
7. Eat healthy foods and make sure to drink water daily.
8. Breathe in through your nose and out through your mouth for 15 to 20 minutes.
9. Focus on the thoughts and feelings that have formed in your mind and heart.
10. Put on the whole Armor of God.
11. Mediate on the following scriptures: Galatians 5:1 and Isaiah 54:17.

Chapter 10

E-EVERY

Every day I will live my life with happiness. Every day of my life will be purposeful. Every day I will smile. Every day I will be kind. Every day, I will speak positivity over my life. Every day I will choose life and every day I will choose me.

The word **every** is defined as all things. There is not a second of the day that should pass by that you cannot account for. Remember the saying, "Idle hands are the devil's playground?" Well, that saying has some truth to it. It means people who waste time doing nothing will eventually be led into sin. 2 Thessalonians 3:11 stated "Yet we hear that some of you are living idle lives, refusing to work and meddling in other people's business." Remember, this is your season, and you must be ready.

The enemy is going to try and attack you by any means necessary. When the enemy realizes that he can't go through you, he will try to attack you through what you love and who you love.

You are stronger than everything the enemy tries to destroy. The armor of God is your protection. When God is for you, does it matter who is against you?

Pray over your children, your home, and for your loved ones. The enemy wants you back and he can't have you because you belong to the Almighty. Continue your journey towards healing and look to the heavens for your answers.

Every day you are given new mercies and grace. Ephesians 2:8-10 says, "God saved you by His grace when you believed. And you can't take credit for this; it is a gift from God. Salvation is not a reward for the good things we have done, so none of us can boast about it. For we are God's masterpiece. He has created us in Christ Jesus, so we can do the good things he planned for us long ago."

I say to you, your thoughts are not your own; however, you are given free will to choose. Become strong in your faith so there is no wavering in your mind and heart. You are on a path that the enemy doesn't want for you. Obstacles will get in your way more than you could imagine; however, you will overcome them all. You have already overcome the biggest obstacles there was: You! Your journey is destined, and your book was already written in Heaven.

PRAYER

Lord God, You are awesome. You are wonderful. You are magnificent. You are Jehovah Jireh, my Prince of Peace.

I worship You because of who you are. I love you! Oh Lord, please continue to fill me up. Lord God, show me the way You would have me to go and allow me to have discernment to know the spirits that I come into contact with. Lord, I know this is not the season to knowingly surround myself with false prophets; yet, they are lurking and trying to pull me back.

I declare and decree that there will be no storms I will not conquer. I declare and decree that I will be slow to anger and not let anger get the best of me. I declare and decree that my children will be great in all they do. I declare and decree that my relationships will be positive and strong. I declare and decree that many lives will be changed because I am able to share my own story freely with no regrets.

In Jesus' Mighty Name, Amen.

STEPS

1. Begin your day with prayer and talk to God.
2. Read your positive affirmations daily.
3. Look at yourself in the mirror and smile.
4. Write down what you love about yourself.
5. Work on your short-term goals.
6. Listen to the songs "Gracefully Broken" and "Spirit" by Tasha Cobbs. Allow the words to sink in and stretch you. Allow the songs to minister to you. Receive and listen to these songs daily.
7. Run in place for two minutes at your own speed, do 10 jumping jacks at your own pace.
8. Eat healthy food and snacks, and make sure to drink water daily.
9. Breathe in through your nose and out through your mouth for 20 to 25 minutes.
10. Focus on the thoughts and feelings that have formed in your mind and heart.
11. Continue to put on the Armor of God.
12. Mediate on the previous and new scriptures: Ephesians 2:8-10 "God saved you by His grace when you believed. And you can't take credit for this; it is a gift from God. Salvation is not a reward for the good things we have done, so none of us can boast about it. For we are God's masterpiece. He has created us in Christ Jesus, so we can do the good things he planned for us long ago." 2 Thessalonians 3:11

states, "Yet we hear that some of you are living idle lives, refusing to work and meddling in other people's business."

Chapter 11

A-Aspiration

You can do it. Don't look back. You are beautiful. You will succeed in all your goals. You have won. You are wonderful. You are strong. You are more than a conquer. You will get the job you want. You will follow your passion and it will make room for you.

You obtain the money you want. Your bank account is full and your debt is paid off. You will get the house you want and make it a home. You will be the person you desire to be. You are full of life and you live on purpose. You have the victory. You have the freedom to breathe!

Your hopes and dreams are coming true because you remain obedient to where God has positioned you. Remember, the sacrifice is nothing without obedience. 1 Samuel 15:22 says, "What is more pleasing to the Lord: your burnt offerings and sacrifices or your obedience to his voice? Listen! Obedience is better than sacrifice and submission is better than offering the fat of rams."

Aspiration means the hope or ambition of achieving something. What are your aspirations?

_____

_____

_____

_____

_____

_____

_____

_____

_____

_____

_____

_____

I hope you mentioned what you achieved during this journey to R.E.V.E.A.L. and H.E.A.L. You have made a tremendous step in your life and you cannot stop now. You have come too far, and you have been stretched wide.

The vision that has been created for you is being accomplished and God is pleased with you. You should be proud of every step you have completed. The road was rocky, and at some points damaged, but obedience smoothed the surface. Your purpose will be revealed before you, just continue to write the vision and achieve the mission.

PRAYER

Lord God, please do not leave me. Please allow each step I take to be a step to get closer to You. Lord God, help me to live by Your Word.

Lord, allow me to love with a pure, discerning heart. Protect me from negative thoughts, actions, and words. Lord God, remove any distractions that may hinder my connection with You.

Father, please teach me how to handle all that comes my way. Help me to recognize any opportunities to choose your will over my own. God, I believe You love me for me and I am thankful. I ask that You continue to order my steps in your Word. In Jesus' name, Amen.

STEPS

1. Begin your day with prayer and talk to God.
2. Read your positive affirmations daily.
3. Look at yourself in the mirror and smile.
4. Write down what you love about yourself.
5. Work on your short-term and long-term goals.
6. Listen to the songs "Worth" by Anthony Brown, "No Weapon" by Fred Hammond; and "One on One" by Zacardi Cortez. Allow the words to sink in and stretch you. Allow the songs to minister to you. Receive and listen to these songs daily.
7. Run in place for 4 minutes at your own speed. Do 15 jumping jacks at your own speed. Walk in place for 2 minutes.
8. Breathe in through your nose and out through your mouth for 20 to 25 minutes.
9. Focus on the thoughts and feelings that have formed in your mind and heart.
10. Eat healthy food and snacks and make sure to drink water daily (very important, I had to repeat).
11. Continue to wear the Armor of God.
12. Mediate on the previous and new scriptures: 1 Samuel 15:22 "What is more pleasing to the Lord: your burnt offerings and sacrifices or your obedience to his voice? Listen! Obedience is better than sacrifice and submission is better than offering the fat of rams."

Chapter 12

L-LIVE

You have made it. You achieved your goal. You leaked. You are free. You are safe. You will achieve the mission set before you. You will win.

Living an exciting and fulfilling life comes with a price. Yes, you have paid a price with your trials and tribulations. Revealing was the first step and working towards healing has been the next step.

In the process of healing, know that you must accept the things you cannot change. There is a prayer called the Serenity Prayer. It was used in recovery for people who were addicted to drugs. The prayer was their go-to prayer to strengthen and remind them that they are human, and they will make mistakes; however, they can't allow these mistakes to control who they are and who they are to become.

Know that your past life was not your fault. Know that you have what it takes to continue your journey to heal. Understand that there will be triggers that can make you stop in your tracks; however, this too shall pass.

When you begin to see signs of the enemy, know that you are warring. The enemy is trying to distract you because he knows you are warring against him.

Think about this, when you were living a basic stress-filled life, the devil didn't tempt you because you were right where he wanted you to be. However, when you felt good in your heart and mind, you started reading the Bible more, attending church, singing your favorite gospel music, or just being positive with no negative thoughts. What happened? The devil tried to lure you with alcohol, sex, flirting, money, tempting emails or messages, etc.

Remember, you are happy and free! You have done what you set your mind to do. You are not scared, ashamed, or guilty because you are strong and you stand on the word of God.

Know that we can make our plans, but the Lord determines our steps (Proverbs 16:9). You have come to the end of your journey. Your goal has been completed and your destiny awaits. I would like you to focus on the Serenity Prayer as we close this chapter.

SERENITY PRAYER

God grant me the serenity to accept the things I cannot change; the courage to change the things I can; and wisdom to know the difference. Living one day at a time; enjoying one moment at a time; accepting hardships as the pathway to peace; taking, as He did, this sinful world as it is, not as I would have it; trusting that He will make all things right if I surrender to His Will; that I may be reasonably happy in this life and supremely happy with Him forever in the next.

Amen.

Congratulations!

Stay on the road of healing and remember, "But don't just listen to God's word. You must do what it says. Otherwise, you are only fooling yourselves" James 1:22.

Listen to the song "Seasons" by Donald Lawrence. It's your season!

A NOTE TO THE READER

It's your time. You have completed the easy part, though it seemed like the hardest. Now you must take the time and stabilize your journey.

Your healing is not a one-time mission, it's a process. Remember, through this process there are going to be some ups and downs but know that each day you will discover something new. Understand that obstacles will get in your way and you will overcome.

Because you started this mission, you have embarked on a road not only to succeed but you have joined STOP (standing together overcoming pain), a community of individuals who were just like you and are now walking in their authority to live lives of purpose. Now you are living life with purpose because you allowed yourself to follow the process to recognize and release each episode attacking life 2 help every aspiration live. Welcome to living!

FOOD FOR THOUGHT

Know that you have faced the most difficult aspect of healing yourself and moving forward to the next level of your life. Continue to war for your sanity, peace and love. I don't want you to believe you are fixed, because my dear, you were never broken—you were just pained and abused.

Realize that this process is not for instant gratification. It will take time. With time, patience, work, and consistency, the triggers that you have recognized will no longer be able to control your emotions.

Always know that you have a choice, and you chose to live a happy, healthy, positive, and stable life. Seeking help is a plus to your journey. A Life Coach, therapist, group counseling sessions, or workshops are great. Always keep yourself in the company of those who desire to help you to become the best you that you can be.

Never be ashamed to get the help you need, even if the help is outside of you. Also, know you will have obstacles that come your way—quicker, stronger, and more cunning than ever before. Your old hurt may resurface more than you would like, but the new you will always intervene. Don't let the enemy trick you into believing your old ways and the old you are the way your life should be.

Healing from the inside out is your personal journey. Trust in God and keep the faith! You will overcome every obstacle that tries to get in your way because your mind, body, emotions, and spirit are armed.

MY PRAYER FOR YOU

Father God in the Mighty Name of Jesus, I ask that you cover the journey of my brother and sister in Christ. I ask that You keep them focused on the task at hand and that You keep them grounded in Your Word.

I ask that the familiarity that finds the soul of any old wounds be destroyed and cast out in the name of Jesus. I ask that You heal the psychological hurt that has caused harm and formed injuries throughout each of their lives. I ask You, oh Lord, to heal the memories of their pain so that they will not remain in pain or be filled with anxiety, fear, hatred, depression, anger, or confusion.

Lord God, help them to forgive anyone who hurt, abandoned, or offended them. Help them to release all deeply rooted wounds and walk in complete forgiveness. Lord, please remove the pain that causes them any physical, mental, or emotional illness.

Lord God. here is my heart of purity for Your children: help them to be humble and feel no oppression. Lord, You are their Rock. You are Love. Break all cycles of abuse and destroy any generational curses over their lives. Lord, please rain joy, peace, love, freedom, understanding, happiness, and financial abundance on them and even Me.

In Jesus Mighty Name, Amen.

CONTINUE THE JOURNEY

To continue your journey with
Octavia Bradley, visit her website:

https://reveal2healconsulting.org

Online Services Available

NOTES

NOTES

NOTES

_____

_____

_____

_____

_____

_____

_____

_____

_____

_____

_____

_____

_____

_____

_____

_____

_____

_____

NOTES

NOTES